DIANA
Her Latest Fashions

First English edition published 1984 by Colour Library Books Ltd.
© 1984 Illustrations and text: Colour Library Books Ltd., Guildford, Surrey, England.
Text filmsetting by Acesetters Ltd., Richmond, Surrey, England.
This edition published by Greenwich House, a division of Arlington House, Inc.,
distributed by Crown Publishers, Inc.,
hgfedcba.
Color separations by Reprocolor Llovet, S.A., Barcelona, Spain.
Printed and bound by Rieusset, S.A. in Barcelona, Spain.
ISBN 0 517 453770

DIANA
Her Latest Fashions

Text by
ALISON JANAWAY

Featuring the photography of
DAVID LEVENSON

GREENWICH HOUSE

"People are so stupid over the way Princess Di dresses," wrote Mrs C. Adam from St Helens to her daily paper. "It seems like that old story of the king and his invisible suit. She wears it, so it must be right." The lady has a point. It would be remarkable if someone with even Diana's massive resources did not make the occasional fashion blunder. The Princess herself will never claim to have been right all the time, far less to have pleased everyone on every occasion. But what people are noticing and applauding is the continuing and largely successful freshness of Diana's approach to wearing those clothes which, in cheaper versions at least, are well within the reach of today's fashion-conscious young and not-so-young. Simplicity has been her theme. When a panel of twenty fashion editors recently cast her as the world's most influential woman of fashion today, they described her as "a symbol of the young conservative swing. She is not only the year's overwhelming favourite for her personal elegance, but the inspiration for a sweeping trend away from eccentricity and towards dressing up."

As she enters into the full months of her second pregnancy, many people are looking forward to some of her new ideas in maternity wear. In the meantime she has indeed had a stunningly chic and exciting year, with some new creations which have sent the fashion buffs reeling. "Copy everything she wears," said one, just after her tour of Canada. "She's a walking style book." The recommendation has proved justified. Among the superb new evening gowns that graced the London autumn scene was that startling blue silk dress with its matching ribbon collar and the low, straight neckline. It was a version of the shimmering lilac gown she had worn in New Zealand, and emphasised Diana's liking for the tight waist separating the wide, low bodice from the skirt which flares out into an ankle-length half crinoline. New, too, last autumn was the silk organza ball-gown in green matt silk which left one shoulder completely bare while sporting a huge compensating bow on the other. That also is a modification of another dress – the sexy number in blue which she wore at the Birthright fashion show a year earlier. Another dress in the same class is the glistening white, cream and gold lamé creation by Hachi, first worn in Melbourne, and repeated on two consecutive occasions in this country subsequently – once at Lord and Lady Romsey's ball at Broadlands, and again at the première of *Octopussy* in London. This development in particular shows how forward-looking she is. At Broadlands, it was glaringly evident that while many of the three hundred female guests – mostly Americans – were still copying her earlier inclinations for the crinoline-style evening gown, Diana had already moved on. As an American buying at London's Fashion Week said the following October, "Until the Princess of Wales, British fashion was not our main concern. Now we cannot afford to ignore the London scene."

Needless to say, Diana's idea of a less formal evening engagement is a pop concert, and three such occasions recently have allowed her to try out a greater range of new outfits. Each one has been not only new, but ecstatically received by people who have now come to expect increasingly adventurous ideas from her. At the Duran Duran concert last summer she wore a cool, emerald green silk two-piece, a slinky looking design reflecting her current penchant for drop-waists, and just the job for a warm night in the middle of an unusually steamy summer. Two months later she turned up at an all-stars rock concert in a dazzling silver outfit consisting of a close-fitting jacket with a raised silvery pattern, over a smooth, silk silver-grey skirt. The effect was immediate. Not only had Diana shown that no-one wore silver better than she did, but her choice proved that she had quickly latched on to yet another fashion development – the mixing of rough and smooth textures to achieve a lustrous, contrasting effect.

But perhaps her greatest moment came at the end of February, when she attended a concert given by Genesis at Birmingham. Perhaps we should have known better, but the last thing we expected Diana to wear was a cream tuxedo-style jacket and black trousers, with a white, silk, wing-collared shirt and a bow-tie to complete the dinner-jacket effect. It was a daring venture into the world of men's fashion, and its designer, Margaret Howell, won golden opinions for it. On the night, Diana won wolf-whistles, and proved that, as on her first official engagement in that notorious black evening dress, she still possesses a sense of independence and fun, as well as a hankering after some of the best influences of the Sloane Ranger cult.

Since Diana bought a huge stock of day clothes in 1981 and 1982, she has had less opportunity to experiment. One of her most dependable designers, David Sassoon, said in September, "she has built up a fantastic wardrobe, but is now wearing the same clothes for many functions." Foremost amongst these is the canteloupe-coloured honeymoon two-piece which has now been worn at least five times – the sleeves have been lengthened and shortened again as one of many examples of royal economy and easy adaption to changes in the weather. One correspondent remarked that it was "the most attractive thing in her wardrobe. I am not surprised she's wearing it again and again." The heavy Welsh wool coat she wore on the day she announced her first pregnancy has had several recent outings, as has the superbly chic Cossack-style grey coat, complete with ornate frogging and Astrakhan collar, muff and hat, which she first wore in December 1981.

In between giving these personal favourites an airing, Diana has shown a marked preference for the more distinctly tailored look in the last twelve months. It began with a couple of numbers, consisting of a long straight drape jacket – some called it Teddy Boy styling – over a matching pencil skirt with kick pleats. She wore a vivid red version of the outfit in Shelburne at the beginning of her visit to Canada, and a deep green copy later during the tour. Though it was summer when she wore them, they served as autumn wear back in Britain where the weather was milder in November than in the Maritime Provinces that June. The same autumn, Diana went almost headlong for the stricter cut which has in some quarters been named The Princess Line in her honour. Jacket waists are pinched in, showing off her trim figure to great advantage, while skirts – whether separate or integral – flare out to emphasise the point. Diana now has several two-piece costumes to this design – one of her favourites seems to be the mauve and grey one she wore at Clarence House on the Queen Mother's 83rd birthday – and she has added them to the coat-dress variety which again she popularised almost single-handedly, without waiting for the trend to develop unaided. This useful device for days of uncertain climate allow the fitted coat to be kept buttoned up, even indoors, without looking cumbersome or uncomfortably hot.

Few of Diana's new fashions, if any, have attracted the sort of criticism which pasted some of her early choices, though she has made the occasional mistake. She repeated her old trick of being caught by photographers against the light, without apparently wearing a slip; it happened once in New South Wales, once in Ottawa and once at St Mary's Hospital, London when she visited her sister Sarah who had just had her first child. And for her arrival in Oslo last January she came off the plane wearing a very summery-looking outfit – a seemingly light-weight dress and coat in brilliant cobalt-blue wool – and without either hat or gloves despite sub-zero temperatures and a biting wind. "Not too clever," commented the *Daily Mirror*. But it had no doubt been planned that way, because waiting at the airport were two of King Olav's grandchildren to hand Diana a bunch of matching blue carnations as she set foot on the tarmac. And if her clothes have generally not disappointed, perhaps the Norwegians were justified in feeling slightly let down when she went to a ballet gala in Oslo wearing a scarlet silk and lace dress which, however brilliant, had been seen a time or two before. Even so, she bowled them over. "We have come to expect such a high standard of beauty," said one Norwegian photographer, "but she has left us goggle-eyed."

Diana wasn't caught out by the weather the following month. She came properly prepared for her second skiing holiday in Liechtenstein, and wore a thick wrap-round mohair jacket in blue and grey, over a rainbow-striped sweater, her grey trousers pushed into calf-length leather boots. The following day she appeared on the slopes, zipped neck to ankles in a maroon and white ski suit, patriotically set off by the blue and white of her hat and boots.

This is the sort of occasion which enables Diana to be at her most adventurous with clothes, and therefore which mark out her most memorable fashion experiences. Even better examples of this development showed up during the 1983 polo season, which saw a completely new, informal Diana blossoming into a whole new range of experimental clothes – all of which were a huge success. Top of the pops in a season where slacks – white, yellow and blue-striped – were the clear favourites, were those rust-coloured pedal-pushers, the leg-hugging, cropped and cuffed knickerbockers which revealed a well-turned calf, worn with a cream silk blouse and topped, Sloane Ranger style, with a bold red cardigan slung and knotted over her shoulders. This outfit won universal notice, not just because it was at the same time comfortable and elegant, and looked well on someone of Diana's height and figure, but because it was typical of the comparatively inexpensive gear currently available to those of her admirers who wish to emulate her. There was also her favourite quilted jacket with the small print flowers in red and turquoise, worn over a straight pleated skirt, which on one occasion was belted so tightly that it prematurely sparked off hints of pregnancy.

But Diana's greatest impact on casual wear was in the knitwear department. Two items in particular proclaimed her passion for woollies, even though she admits that she herself can't knit. One was a heavy, dark blue cardigan, illuminated with colourful weather scenes – clouds, sunshine, lightning, rain and a rainbow. "She has summed up the day perfectly," said a member of the London Weather Centre, observing wryly that on that very day the summer heat-wave broke up in a series of storms. But more popular still was the bright red jumper, closely patterned with white sheep motifs, which she had worn over two years earlier for a photocall at Balmoral. Only this time, one – but only one – of the white sheep had been replaced by a black one. That really set the tongues wagging; was she trying to tell us that *she* was the black sheep of the family? Whatever the answer, the design certainly caught on. Six of them were offered as prizes a week later in a newspaper competition – "Who do you think is the black sheep of the Royal Family?" – and by the end of the year, Sally Muir who designed them at her Chelsea shop *Warm and Wonderful*, had sold no fewer than 2,500 of them. They retailed for £60 apiece, which may have seemed expensive but, as Sally explained, they were hand-framed, the knitting machines being operated by hand, and each sweater being hand-shaped and made up. The idea was so popular that by September one of the shop's former staff was sued for selling jumpers featuring sheep on them at her own newly-established premises.

So the innovative, almost dare-devil spirit in which Diana first appeared in public as Prince Charles' fiancée has yet to burn itself out. One refreshing consequence is that she has not fallen into the trap of relying on traditional or well-tried ideas when choosing her clothes for the day. Her two dressers, Valerie Gibbs and Evelyn Dagley, will lay out several outfits practical to the day's events, and Diana will choose from them according to her mood. In doing so, she is no slave to convention. She recently breached the tradition whereby something at least vaguely plaid is worn at the Braemar Games, by choosing a bottle-green coat-dress with brown accessories which owed nothing to the Scottish connections of the rest of the Royal Family. She has no qualms about wearing a dress twice in quick succession – like the turquoise wool coat she wore on Christmas day 1981 and again at Tulse Hill on her first public outing of 1982; or the glowing pink outfit worn at the wedding of her friend Sophie Kimball one day in November 1982, again for the State Visit of the Queen of the Netherlands the next day, and yet again the following month at Windsor. She refuses to follow the age-old royal custom of wearing brooches, and on the rare occasions when she has to wear flowers – poppies during Remembrance Week for instance, and oak-leaves for a Founder's Day visit to the Chelsea Pensioners, she prefers to pin them to her right side rather than, as is the custom, to the left.

Just now and then she will concede fashion to the occasion, as for her arrival in Canada when, for the first and only time to date, she wore a dress which reflected the colours of the Maple Leaf flag. And on the same tour she was game enough to join in the fun at the Fort Edmonton Klondike-style entertainment, by turning up in high Victorian period costume, complete with bustle, lace bonnet, high boots and parasol. There was even whalebone ribbing in the bodice of the dress, and she freely admitted the following day that she was glad to be back in ordinary clothes again.

In her choice of accessories, Diana has given a much-needed boost to several home manufacturing and service industries. The low-heeled pumps that once upon a time were scarcely available to any girl even marginally outside the average footsize, suddenly popped up everywhere when she came onto the scene. Interestingly, she wears higher heels only when she carries out solo engagements; the stumpier variety are produced when Prince Charles accompanies her, so as to keep her looking slightly less tall than him. Diana is only one and a half inches shorter than her husband, so the height of heels has to be watched carefully. Her hats are still a great success. By not wearing them as a matter of course, she emphasises the use to which they can be put. She cannot claim to wear a very comprehensive variety of type of hat – after all, the vast majority do come from one designer, John Boyd. But her almost unerring eye for the jaunty feather or breezy veil have rescued these ornamentations from what once seemed certain obscurity and disfavour. She has held fast to the small, envelope-designed clutch bag, whether in leather or suede for day wear, or soft or shiny fabric for evening events, at the expense of the handbag. If she carries a larger bag at all, she prefers one that can be slung over the shoulder. The reason again is practical – the clutch bag can be tucked under the arm, or the shoulder bag hitched out of the way to leave both hands free for accepting the huge amounts of flowers and gifts offered to her in the course of every walkabout.

Stockings, or more regularly tights, are worn essentially for comfort. She told guests at one charity dinner that Prince Charles had asked her not to wear them in warm weather, and on the whole she doesn't. She dispensed with them during her three days in Alice Springs, and even attended a Buckingham Palace garden party bare-legged. That was at the height of the heat-wave, and those ladies who deferred to what was considered more correct dress sweltered almost painfully through the afternoon, while Diana sailed through the proceedings in relative comfort. When she does choose to wear them, she can pick from a vast accumulation of styles. She is the first lady of the Royal Family to wear coloured tights, and as early as November 1981 was seen in a pair of the opaque cream-coloured variety which became popular that winter. She then progressed to lacy, delicately-patterned tights, though an even later development – non see-through *and* patterned – met with disapproval: "nasty pale glitter tights," one observer called them. How different from her much more recent sally into a little extravagance which may well start a stampede. Nobody's calves and ankles were photographed quite as much as hers when, on a visit to a police training college at Hendon late in March 1984, she wore tights – or was it stockings? – with pronounced back-seams culminating in a pretty butterfly-bow motif at the heel. Their Italian style, revived from the late fifties by Pierre Mantoux of Milan, had already been featured at various Paris fashion shows, but only when Diana bought them from Harvey Nichols of Knightsbridge, did they cause such a public sensation. Within two days, major London stores were having to turn away the flood of customers for want of stock. "There hadn't been a real demand for them before," said a John Lewis spokesman, "but we have had quite a rush today." They also gave one rampant male reason to hope that "perhaps we shall see fewer women hiding trim ankles in boots, trousers and leg-warmers."

Diana now owns about two million pounds worth of jewellery, much of it, in value terms at least, acquired at the time of her wedding. But even three years later, she is no ostentatious wearer of gems. Even on State occasions, the royal ladies' perennial excuse for sporting the very best from the Palace vaults, Diana opts for simple combinations of sparkling pieces. A tiara is obligatory, so she matches one of her two possessions with a delicate pair of earrings and perhaps a light, unfussy necklace. Otherwise, she can afford to wear slightly heavier jewellery, but with her fine and slender figure, she has wisely chosen not to follow the Queen and Queen Mother with their very weighty, large-stoned royal heirlooms. Because she is not slow to use her enviable collection of jewellery even for casual wear, Diana has given a new lease of life to the concept of young people wearing family gems, and her contemporaries are seeking out the most suitable of their parents' antique jewellery, to give them a timely airing. For the less well-off, Diana has provided some useful leads in her choice of small, unobtrusive items, such as pendants and slim bracelets, for everyday or casual wear. One of her recent favourites has been the fine gold necklace with a large flat medallion pendant bearing the name William in Prince Charles' handwriting, and which is thought to have been a 22nd birthday present from her husband.

With the undoubted success of the 1982 experiment in liberating the pregnant Princess from the traditional royal constraints on public appearance, it is on the cards that we shall see much more of Diana as she awaits her second child. It will be interesting to see what changes she makes to her very informal, almost utilitarian maternity wardrobe of two years ago to satisfy the greater expectations we have of her as one who, to quote designer Sassoon, "has given Britain the most exciting fashion image in the world."

Two versions of Diana's favourite pill-box hat (right) show her love of veils and bows. Frills have been her constant hallmark: the evening dress (below) is lace-frilled at collar, sleeve and waist. (Bottom pictures) making the most of long legs: one of Diana's smartest casual outfits in 1983.

While vivid colours make it easier for Diana to be spotted even when engulfed by crowds, she has experimented with pastel shades as well. The clouds and flower design (below) has proved a great favourite.

No doubt about the success of this striking black and white blouse, seen (below) at Smith's Lawn in the summer of 1983. Diana had previously worn it to a disco evening in Adelaide, South Australia. For more formal occasions, the high collar, either on blouse (right) or on jacket (left, centre) substitutes for the more usual ruffle. Notice the unusual cameo pinning the silk blouse (bottom left). Diana's love of antique jewellery has sent many of her aristocratic contemporaries searching through family treasures for suitable revivals.

(Left) Diana's loyalty to her going-away outfit continues unabated. Its sleeves have been lengthened and shortened again, its waist taken in to fit her slimmer figure. Jewellery is usually kept to a minimum: a single row of pearls (right and bottom left) emphasises her theme of simplicity. Even the three-strand choker (bottom centre) is almost lost on her. (Bottom right) one of Diana's newest daytime outfits, the brilliant cobalt-blue set with the dazzling, striped cravat-style collar.

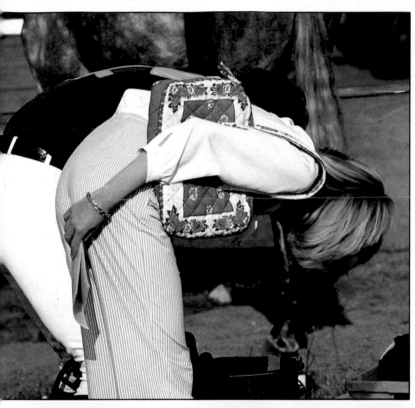

(Opposite page) not only new but popular: Diana's blue coat again, matching her eyes and the dyed carnations presented to her when she arrived in Oslo in January 1984. Two less familiar evening dresses: (far left) the frilled tube-top first worn in the autum of 1982 and only seen once since; (left) the beautifully-proportioned blue-green one-shouldered gown with its splashy bow. Some found the traditional crinoline skirt and the novel drop waist difficult to appreciate.

A good mixer: Diana can't please all the people all the time, but there is something for everyone in this selection of styles.

(Right) Diana performing a good turn – mainly for the photographers who flocked to Liechtenstein to see her on the ski-slopes. Maroon seemed to suit her here, but she rarely wears it when on duty.

Even though best-suited by bright or soft colours, Diana's use of crisp white collars and cuffs makes even drab colours stand out (bottom left).

The familiar wool coat (far left) has been seen several times since Diana announced her first pregnancy. Yet to establish itself is this smart outfit (centre left) with its space-age hat and blood-red kerchief, first worn on Christmas Day 1983.

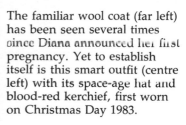

(Above) one of the floaty, summer outfits for which Diana has been well-known and (left) the more severely tailored look which heralded her autumn fashions of 1983. (Opposite) one of Diana's newest cocktail dresses: note again the penchant for the dropped waist.

A head for hats. Diana in a selection of stylish headgear: (right) the famous John Boyd straw tricorne with its generous ostrich-feather flourish; (far right) the flat pillbox for vibrantly coloured outfits; (bottom left) the chic, wide-brimmed hat with its rich satin-finish band. (Opposite) a casual, yet elegant wool dress made these Christmas 1983 pictures of Diana with Prince William and Prince Charles especially homely. William's ABC suit became instantly as popular as many of his mother's clothes have been.

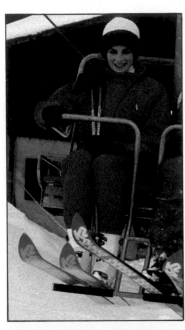

Diana prefers to carry a small clutch bag (bottom picture) on official engagements, though occasionally a shoulder bag (opposite page) will provide an alternative. Bigger bags (below) are reserved for more informal occasions.

Diana has revived the Edwardian look with her tight-fitting neckwear. The choker most readily associated with her (bottom right) is a smaller example of a seven-strand version she sometimes wears. The emerald and platinum band (right) compliments a low-cut dress.

Diana is the first female member of the Royal Family to demonstrate that hats are by no means compulsory. She has a canny sense of the degree of formality involved at any official event, and decides about headgear accordingly.

Generally, Diana favours small designs on her clothes. The polka-dot craze of the Fifties is reflected in many of her dresses, while larger disc and ring designs are becoming more frequent. The butterfly and dragonfly patterned dress (far right) became a winner both in Australia and back home.

Diana's liking for tinted hosiery is another royal novelty. Not since the days of Princess Anne's colourful hats have British fashions become so significant.

These pictures seem to explain why Diana went to such great lengths to slim after Prince William's birth. Her slick tuxedo-style outfit for the Genesis concert at Birmingham early in 1984 (opposite page) was particularly well suited to her slender figure.

(Below and bottom centre) two superb evening gowns. The scarlet one is possibly her favourite, and she wore it when sitting for an official portrait unveiled in 1984.

Diana's hairstyle has been modified almost imperceptibly in the last two years. Her latest experiment involved curling her hair at the side and flicking it back. She still has her hair highlighted.

(Left, below, and bottom) three of Diana's favourites – the multicoloured Welsh wool coat was first seen in 1981; the heavily-patterned ensemble in 1982, and the bright blue coat in 1984. (Right and opposite page) Diana seemed to find polo much more watchable in 1983 than she had the previous year.

(Above) the zoot-suit, which Diana first wore in Canada. (Far right) a natty wool suit, first seen in Autum 1982, which sports contrasting rough and smooth textures. (Top right) a leaf from the Queen's book: Diana's hat has a trembling-feather ornamentation popularised by both the Queen and Princess Anne.

Despite her height, Diana keeps her look of delicacy by avoiding heavy jewellery. For day wear, earrings are usually worn on a clip, though even drops (below) are kept close to the ear. Bracelets are similarly unobtrusive (far left and bottom) and rings, apart from her huge sapphire and diamond engagement ring, plain. One of her gold rings is a small-scale replica of Prince Charles' crested signet ring.

Though she looks stunning in ultra feminine clothes, the deep-lapelled jacket style is becoming increasingly popular with Diana. The more obvious Teddy Boy style (bottom) is more subtly reflected in the silver-grey quilted jacket (far right) with its silk blouse bow.

A breezy reception on alighting from a helicopter (top right) highlights the dangers of hatlessness. (Top left) a perfect picture of Diana's new coiffure, with the hair rolled to give a more rounded and full-bodied appearance.

(Opposite page) a happy picture of Diana, which shows how little make-up she needs. "She blushes very prettily", her cosmetician once said of her. "Those blushes should be allowed to shine through."

Unlike the last two Princesses of Wales, Diana can boast only two tiaras. This one (opposite) was a gift from the Queen.